PRAYING WITH PURPOSE:
UNREACHED PEOPLES

WRITTEN AND COMPILED BY
Barbara (Tommi) Femrite

*Ask of Me and I will give you the nations as your
inheritance, and the uttermost parts of
the earth for your possession.*
Psalm 2:8 AMP

**CANOPY
PRESS**
Bulverde, Texas

PRAYING WITH PURPOSE:
UNREACHED PEOPLES

By Barbara (Tommi) Femrite

Copyright © 1997; Revised © 1999
By Intercessors International
Bulverde, Texas

Cover Design By Keith Sherrer

ISBN 0-9620378-6-9

Intercessors International
P.O. Box 390
Bulverde, Texas 78163 USA
(830) 438-2615

This work is dedicated to

MY INHERITANCE

The Bride living in darkness who has not yet heard
the glorious Gospel of Jesus Christ —

THE UNREACHED PEOPLES OF THE WORLD

Arise, shine, for your light has come!
Isaiah 60:1

PREFACE

The sun beat down on our small group of musicians and intercessors as we stood in the midst of sand dunes. We had come from several nations to worship the King of Kings and the Lord of Lords in the heart of the Gobi Desert.

Suddenly it became a reality to me—Mongolia was part of the Bride of Christ. She was unable to sing the love song to her Bridegroom. We stood in her place singing for the Bride until she can sing for herself.

Shouts of proclamations to the nation rose from my lips. "I declare that you are part of the Bride! No longer will you be found naked! No longer will you be ashamed when you stand before the Lord on that great judgment day! For you have been clothed in garments of white! I call you as the Bride! I call you to take your rightful place beside your Bridegroom! Be free, Mongolia! Be free!"

The Word of the Lord goes forth like fire and a hammer, consuming the enemy and shattering the obstacles he has placed before the nations of the 10/40 Window. Ninety-five percent of the least evangelized people in the world live in this geographical area. Unreached peoples have never had the opportunity of hearing the Gospel for the first time. Satan has blinded their eyes and held them in darkness for centuries.

Around the world Christians are uniting in strategic prayer efforts in order to penetrate this darkness with the light of Christ.

The Lord has made us His war club, His weapon for battle. We have been anointed to open blind eyes, set captives free and release those who sit in darkness.

Together we are declaring to the unreached people groups, *"The light has dawned on those living in the land of the shadow of death. Arise, shine, for your light has come!"* (Isaiah 9:2; 60:1).

Jesus said, *"My house shall be called a house of prayer for all peoples"* (Mark 11:17). Our prayers will make a difference in the lives of the unreached people groups of the world. Millions of intercessors are standing in the gap as watchmen on the wall for these unreached people groups until they can stand with us.

One day we will join with them and stand around the throne of God singing, *"To Him who sits on the throne and unto the Lamb be blessing and honor and glory and power, for ever and ever! Amen."* (Revelation 5:12,13 NAS).

Thy kingdom come, Thy will be done.
Matthew 6:10 NAS

TABLE OF CONTENTS

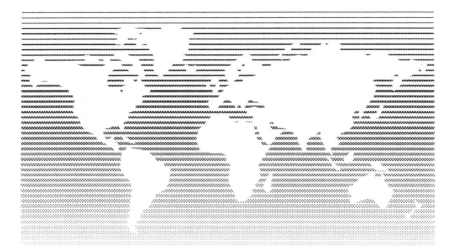

How To Use This Book

The prayers in this book have been written using scriptures. Eight different topics are provided to help focus your prayer efforts. As you pray, insert the name of the unreached people group for whom you are praying.

The Word of God comes alive in your mouth as you pray these prayers in an audible voice and proclaim His glory to the nations. Whether you pray through *Praying With Purpose: Unreached Peoples* in one sitting, pray one topic or choose selected scriptures from each topic, God watches over His Word and is faithful to fulfill it. Before you begin, take a few minutes to prepare your heart before the Lord.

You may choose to pray alone, with a prayer partner or a group of intercessors. Perhaps you will take a prayer journey. Bring copies of *Praying With Purpose: Unreached Peoples* for each member of the team. This way you each have scriptures at your finger tips to proclaim over the land. Use the blank pages provided in the back to record additional topics and scriptures.

I have taken this book on many prayer journeys. It was so convenient to have it with me as I walked through the streets of Haridwar, India. Pilgrims had come to dip in the Ganges River believing their sins would be washed away. My prayers focused on the topic *Cleanse Their Hearts*. Perched on a watchtower on the Great Wall of China, I found myself proclaiming these prayers in a loud voice over the nations of China and Mongolia. After pouring scripture into the atmosphere in Romania, my team left our copies with missionaries. They will continue to proclaim the Word over the land.

Consider praying these prayers for those in government, education, law enforcement, business, armed forces, media, sports, etc. Reach the unreached leaders through your prayers and see the Word change their lives.

Intercessors International encourages you to use other prayer tools in conjunction with *PRAYING WITH PURPOSE: UNREACHED PEOPLES* to enhance your prayer time. A list of recommended reading material has been included. When using the *Praying Through The Window Prayer Calendar,* which lists nations for each day of the month, instead of inserting one people group in the blank, insert the designated nations for the date you are praying.

For more detailed information, a listing of organizations and ministries is included to assist you in your intercession. These groups can provide you with data which will give you additional insight when praying for a specific unreached people group.

Intercessors International has several teaching tapes to further train, encourage and support you in this endeavor. These are listed in the back and you may order them directly from our office.

Proclaim My glory among the nations.
Isaiah 66:19

LIGHT THE WINDOW

During the worship service the Sunday before Intercessors International departed on a prayer journey for the Gond people in India, I had a vision of the 10/40 Window with layers of curtains over it. The first curtain was a *blackout shade* like the kind used during the war. This curtain totally blacked out all the light. I saw that this curtain had been removed—it had been lifted through prayer.

The second curtain was *opaque*. Light could be detected but I could not see people, places or faces. There was only the indication of light. This, too, had been removed—it had been lifted through prayer.

The third curtain was *translucent*. Light shined through even brighter. I could see movement and forms but could not make out faces or details. Then I saw people from around the world holding cords to this curtain. The Lord was ready to give His command to lift this curtain, to remove the canopy, to lift the veil.

And, as we pulled together through prayer, His light and His glory began to shine through the Window.

In thinking about these curtains, I believe they have been removed through the *Praying Through the Window I, II* and *III* efforts. I know there is a fourth curtain. It is *transparent.* Light flows through it so that the people, places and faces may be seen distinctly. This curtain must also be lifted. It stands between the Lord and the people of the 10/40 Window—between the Lord and His Bride, who yet lives in darkness. We must join together, pulling the cords to this curtain through prayer to let Jesus, the Light of the world, shine brightly on each face.

My expectations run high for *Praying Through the Window IV.* May the Lord's glory and presence shine brightly on the peoples and nations of the 10/40 Window.

LET ALL THE PEOPLES PRAISE YOU

Father, I come boldly and with confidence before Your throne of grace today to stand in the gap for the (name) people. Lord, You have posted me as a watchman on the walls of the (name) people. I will never be silent, day or night. I will call on You, Lord, and give You no rest till You establish the (name) people and make them the praise of the earth. (Hebrews 4:16; Ezekiel 22:30; Isaiah 62:6,7)

I ask You for the (name) people as my inheritance and possession. With confidence, I will lift up my voice and not be afraid to say to the (name) people, "Here is your God!" (Psalm 2:8; Isaiah 40:9)

Lord, You are awesome, the great King over all the (name) people. You chose our inheritance for us. I sing praises to You, my God and King, for You are King over all the (name) people. You reign over the (name) people. (Psalm 47:2-8)

You revealed Yourself to those who did not ask for You and You were found by those who did not seek You. To the (name) people that did not call on Your name, You said, "Here am I, here am I." (Isaiah 65:1)

I ask that the (name) people would be still, and know that You are God. You, O Lord, will be exalted among the (name) people. You, O Lord, will be exalted in the earth. For the earth is Yours and everything in it, the world, and all the (name) people. Rise up, O God, for the (name) people are Your inheritance. (Psalms 46:10; 24:1; 82:8)

Sovereign Lord, You have made the heavens and the earth by Your great power and outstretched arm. Nothing is too hard for You. You show love to thousands. O great and powerful God, whose name is the Lord Almighty, great are Your purposes for the (name) people and mighty are Your deeds. Your eyes are open to all the ways of the (name) people. (Jeremiah 32:17-19)

All the earth bows down to You. They sing praise to You. They sing praise to Your name. I pray the (name) people will come and see what God has done. How awesome are Your works on their behalf. You rule forever by Your power and Your eyes watch over the (name) people. (Psalm 66:4-7)

I pray the (name) people will praise You, Lord. May their souls know You as their very great God. May they see You clothed with splendor and majesty. I will praise You, O Lord, among the (name) people. I will sing of You among the (name) people and proclaim to them what You have done. (Psalms 104:1; 108:3; 9:11)

I declare Your glory among the (name) people, Your marvelous deeds among all peoples. For You are great and most worthy of praise. You are to be feared above all gods. For You, O Lord, are the Most High over all the (name) people. You are exalted far above all gods. (Psalms 96:3,4; 97:9)

Be exalted, O God, above the heavens, and let Your glory be over all the (name) people. You, Lord, are exalted over all the (name) people, Your glory above the heavens. O Lord, You are exalted forever. (Psalms 108:5; 113:4; 92:8)

May the (name) people praise You, O God. May all the (name) people praise You. May the (name) people be glad and sing for joy, for You rule and guide them justly. May the (name) people praise You. (Psalm 67:3-5)

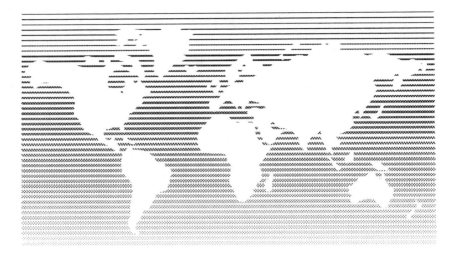

LET YOUR LIGHT SHINE

Lord, You sent Jesus as a witness to testify concerning the light, so that the (name) people might believe in it, adhere to it, trust it, and rely upon it through Him. This light is a revelation to the (name) people declaring: You are light and in You there is no darkness at all. (John 1:7 AMP; Luke 2:32; 1 John 1:5)

Father, I pray the (name) people would arise and shine, for their light has come, and the glory of the Lord has risen upon them. For darkness covers the earth and a thick darkness is over the (name) people, but You, Lord, rise upon the (name) people and Your glory appears over them. I pray the (name) people will come to Your light, and kings to the brightness of Your dawn. As the (name) people assemble together and lift up their eyes, may their faces be radiant and their hearts throb and swell with joy. (Isaiah 60:1-5)

17

O Lord, the gospel has been veiled to the (name) people who are perishing. The god of this age has blinded the minds of the (name) people, so that they cannot see the light of the gospel of the glory of Christ. Lord, when You said, "Let light shine out of darkness," You made Your light shine in the hearts of the (name) people and gave them the light of the knowledge of the glory of God in the face of Christ. (2 Corinthians 4:3-6)

I pray as the (name) people walk in the light, as You are in the light, that they will have fellowship with one another, and the blood of Jesus, Your Son, will purify them from all sin. Lord, they claim to be without sin, having deceived themselves and the truth is not in them. I pray they would confess their sins, for You are faithful and just and will forgive their sins and purify them from all unrighteousness. (1 John 1:7-9)

Father, it is my prayer that You will lead the (name) people by ways they have not known and that You will guide them along unfamiliar paths. Father God, turn the darkness into light before the (name) people and make the rough places smooth, for You have promised You will do it and that You will not forsake them. (Isaiah 42:16)

May the (name) people walk in the light of the Lord. May they come to know Jesus as the light of the world, for whoever follows Him will never walk in darkness, but will have the light of life. (Isaiah 2:5; John 8:12)

Father, I ask that You would open the eyes of the (name) people and turn them from darkness to light, and from the power of Satan to You, so that they may receive forgiveness of sins and a place among those who are sanctified. (Acts 26:18)

I pray that the (name) people walking in darkness will see a great light, for Your word declares that the light has dawned on those living in the land of the shadow of death. I thank You, Lord, that You will be their everlasting light and glory. May the day of sorrow of the (name) people come to an end. (Isaiah 9:2; 60:19,20; Matthew 4:16)

You, Lord, have chosen the (name) people. They are a royal priesthood, a holy nation, a people belonging to You, God. I pray the (name) people will declare praises to You who called them out of darkness into Your wonderful light. (1 Peter 2:9)

Thank You, Father, that Light has come to the (name) people. I pray they live by the truth and come into the light. You are the One who turns their darkness into light. When You created the world, You spoke and said, "Let there be light," and there was light. Let the light of Your face shine upon the (name) people, O Lord. (John 3:19-21; Psalm 18:28; Genesis 1:3; Psalm 4:6)

Cleanse Their Hearts

Father, I pray the (name) people, who are called by Your name, will humble themselves and pray and seek Your face and turn from their wicked ways, for then You will hear from heaven and will forgive their sin and will heal their land. (2 Chronicles 7:14)

Lord, beckon the (name) people to come and reason together with You. May the sins of the (name) people which are like scarlet be as white as snow. Even though they are red as crimson, make them like wool. (Isaiah 1:18,19)

For the sake of Your name, O Lord, forgive the iniquity of the (name) people, though it is great. (Psalm 25:11)

Father, in Your love keep the (name) people from the pit of destruction and put their sins behind Your back. Sovereign Lord, wipe away the tears from all their faces and remove the disgrace of the (name) people. (Isaiah 38:17; 25:8)

I ask, Father, that You would sprinkle clean water on the (name) people so they will be clean. Cleanse the (name) people from all their impurities and from all their idols. Give the (name) people a new heart and put a new spirit in them. Lord, remove the heart of stone from the (name) people and give them a heart of flesh. Put Your Spirit in the (name) people and move them to follow Your decrees and keep Your laws. (Ezekiel 36:25-27)

Lord, I tenderly speak comfort to the (name) people and proclaim to them that their hard service has been completed. I thank You that the sin of the (name) people has been paid for. (Isaiah 40:1,2)

I thank You that the blood of Christ cleanses the consciences of the (name) people from acts that lead to death so that they may serve the living God! (Hebrews 9:14)

Merciful God, I thank You that repentance and forgiveness of sins will be preached in Your name to all the (name) people. (Luke 24:47)

Lord, I thank You, that You will bring health and healing to the (name) people. You will help them and will let them enjoy abundant peace and security. Thank You that You will bring the (name) people back from captivity and will rebuild them. Thank You that You will cleanse them from all the sin they have committed against You and will forgive all their sins of rebellion. (Jeremiah 33:6-8)

Lord Jesus, You are worthy to take the scroll and to open its seals, because You were slain, and with Your blood You purchased men for God from every tribe and language and people and nation. I thank You, Father, that You have made the (name) people to be a kingdom and priests to serve You and that they will reign on the earth. (Revelation 5:9,10)

RESTORE THEM UNTO YOU

Father, I thank You that as the (name) people wait patiently for You, that You will turn to them and hear their cry. Lord, I ask that You would lift them out of the slimy pit, out of the mud and mire. Set the feet of the (name) people on a rock and give them a firm place to stand. Put a new song in the mouths of the (name) people, a hymn of praise to You, God. May the (name) people see and fear and put their trust in You, Lord. (Psalm 40:1-3)

I pray the (name) people will praise You, Lord; that their souls, their inmost beings, would praise Your holy name. I ask that the (name) people not forget Your benefits. Father, You forgive all the sins of the (name) people and heal all of their diseases. You are the One who redeems their lives from the pit and You crown the (name) people with love and compassion. Lord, I ask that You would satisfy their desires with good things and that their youth would be renewed like the eagle's. (Psalm 103:1-5)

Lord, build up the (name) people, gather them, heal their broken hearts, bind up their wounds and cure their pains and their sorrows. Father, You are close to the brokenhearted and save those who are crushed in spirit. (Psalm 147:2-6 AMP; 34:18)

Father, I ask when the (name) people cry to You in their trouble that You will save them from their distress. Send forth Your word and heal them. Rescue the (name) people from the grave. I pray the (name) people will give thanks to You for Your unfailing love and Your wonderful deeds for them. May the (name) people offer thanks to You and tell of Your works with songs of joy. (Psalm 107:19-22)

I pray the (name) people will not be afraid and that they will not suffer shame. O Lord, do not let them fear disgrace nor be humiliated. Father, let them forget the shame of their youth and remember no more the reproach of their widowhood. Lord Almighty, You are the Maker and Husband of the (name) people. You are the Holy One, the Redeemer of the (name) people and their God. I thank You, Lord, that You have called the (name) people back as if they were a wife deserted and distressed in spirit, a wife who married young, only to be rejected. For a brief moment You abandoned the (name) people, but with deep compassion You will bring them back. In a surge of anger You hid Your face from the (name) people for a moment, but with everlasting kindness You will have compassion on the (name) people. (Isaiah 54:4-8)

For the (name) people's sake I will not keep silent, for the (name) people's sake I will not remain quiet, till her righteousness shines like the dawn, her salvation like a blazing torch. The nations will see the (name) people's righteousness, and all the kings their glory. The (name) people will be called by a new name that You have given them. I pray the (name) people will be a crown of splendor, a royal diadem in Your hand, Lord. May the (name) people no longer be called Deserted, or their land Desolate for You delight in them and rejoice over them. (Isaiah 62:1-4)

Dear Lord, I agree with your invitation to the (name) people to come to You, all of them who are weary and burdened, for You will give them rest. I pray the (name) people would take Your yoke upon them and learn from You, for You are gentle and humble in heart, and they will find rest for their souls. For Your yoke is easy and Your burden is light. (Matthew 11:28-30)

Lord, I ask that You would wipe every tear from the eyes of the (name) people. Take away their crying and pain. You, O Lord, are compassionate and gracious. You are slow to anger and abounding in love and faithfulness. (Revelation 21:4; Psalm 86:15)

Father, may the (name) people come and bow down and worship and kneel before You, their Maker, for You are their God and they are the people of Your pasture, the flock under Your care. May the (name) people hear Your voice today and not harden their hearts. (Psalm 95:6-8)

Lord, tend to the (name) people like a shepherd tends to his flock. Gather the (name) people as lambs in Your arms and carry them close to Your heart. Gently lead those that have young. (Isaiah 40:11)

I pray the (name) people would not be afraid, for You are with them; You will bring their children from the east and gather them from the west. You will say to the north, "Give them up!" and to the south, "Do not hold them back." (Isaiah 43:5,6)

LET YOUR KINGDOM COME

Father, You know the thoughts and plans You have for the (name) people. These are thoughts and plans for welfare and peace, not for evil, to give them hope in their final outcome. I pray that the (name) people will call upon You, and that they will come and pray to You, and that You will hear them. Then the (name) people will seek You as a vital necessity and find You; when they search for You with all their heart, they will find You. Lord, release the (name) people from their captivity and gather them from all the nations and all the places You have driven them. (Jeremiah 29:11-14 AMP)

I pray that all the (name) people will remember and turn to You and that all the families of the (name) people will bow down before You, for dominion belongs to You, Lord, and You rule over the (name) people. (Psalm 22:27,28)

May the (name) people turn to You, Lord, and be saved for You are God, and there is no other. You have sworn by Yourself, the word is gone out of Your mouth in righteousness and will not turn back. O Lord, may every knee of the (name) people bow and every tongue of the (name) people give praise to You and confess that Jesus Christ is Lord. (Isaiah 45:22,23 NAS; Romans 10:9)

No one is like You, O Lord; You are great, and Your name is mighty in power. Who should not revere You, O King of the (name) people? This is Your due. Among all the wise men of the nations and in all their kingdoms, there is no one like You. (Jeremiah 10:6,7)

I pray the (name) people will be full of the knowledge of You, Lord, as the waters cover the sea. Let Your kingdom come to the (name) people. Let Your will be done in the hearts of the (name) people. (Isaiah 11:9; Matthew 6:10)

I pray that all the (name) people You have made will come and worship before You, O Lord, and that they will bring glory to Your name. For You are great and do marvelous deeds. You alone are God. (Psalm 86:9,10)

Lord, You make Your salvation known and reveal Your righteousness to the (name) people. May the (name) people praise and extol You, Lord. For great is Your love towards the (name) people and Your faithfulness and love endures forever. (Psalms 98:2; 117:1,2; 118:1)

O God, open a door for the message, so that we may proclaim the mystery of Christ to the (name) people. I have opened my eyes and looked at the fields. They are ripe for harvest. The harvest is plentiful but the workers are few. Lord of the harvest, send out workers into Your harvest field. (Colossians 4:3; John 4:35; Matthew 9:37,38)

Glorious Father, give the (name) people the Spirit of wisdom and revelation in the deep, intimate, full knowledge of You. May the eyes of the (name) people's hearts be flooded with light, so that they can know and understand the hope to which You have called them. May the (name) people know how rich Your glorious inheritance is in the saints. I pray the (name) people can know and understand what is the immeasurable and unlimited and surpassing greatness of Your power for us who believe. (Ephesians 1:17-19 AMP)

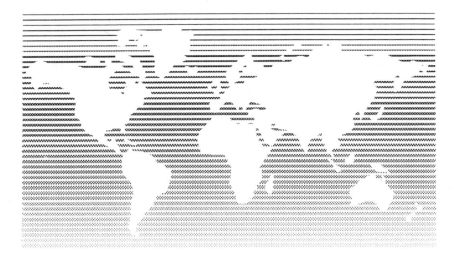

YOUR NAME IS GREAT

Lord, Your name will be great among the (name) people, from the rising to the setting of the sun. In every place incense and pure offerings will be brought to Your name, because Your name will be great among the (name) people. (Malachi 1:11)

O God, show the holiness of Your great name, which has been profaned among the (name) people. I thank You that nations will know that You are the Sovereign Lord when You show Yourself holy through the (name) people before their eyes. (Ezekiel 36:23)

I pray the (name) people will fear Your name, Lord, and that all the kings of the earth will revere Your glory. (Psalm 102:15)

May Your name endure forever; may it continue as long as the sun. The (name) people will be blessed through You and they will call You blessed. I praise You, Lord God, the God of the (name) people, who alone does marvelous deeds. I praise Your glorious name forever; may the (name) people be filled with Your glory. (Psalm 72:17-19)

Father, I thank You that You exalted Jesus to the highest place and gave Him the name that is above every name, that at the name of Jesus every knee should bow, in heaven and on earth and under the earth, and every tongue confess that Jesus Christ is Lord, to the glory of God the Father. (Philippians 2:9-11)

I thank You, Lord, that salvation is found in no one else, for there is no other name under heaven given to men by which we must be saved. I pray the (name) people will call on the name of the Lord and be saved. (Acts 4:12; Romans 10:13)

Father, I praise You that the (name) people along with a great multitude from every nation, tribe, people and language will be standing before the throne and in front of the Lamb. They will be wearing robes and holding palm branches in their hands. Lord, I rejoice that the (name) people will cry out in a loud voice: "Salvation belongs to our God, who sits on the throne, and to the Lamb." (Revelation 7:9,10)

I pray the families of the (name) people will ascribe to You, Lord, glory and strength and that they will ascribe the glory due Your name. May the (name) people worship You in the splendor of Your holiness and tremble before You. For the (name) people will say among the nations, "The Lord reigns." (Psalm 96:7-10)

Let the (name) people be glad. Let them rejoice. Clouds and thick darkness surround You; righteousness and justice are the foundation of Your throne. Fire goes before You and consumes Your foes on every side. Your lightning lights up the world; the (name) people see and tremble. The mountains melt like wax before You, for You are Lord of all the (name) people. The heavens proclaim Your righteousness, and all the (name) people see Your glory. (Psalm 97:1-6)

I pray that You, O Lord, will shake the (name) people so that they will come and fill Your house with glory. (Haggai 2:7)

OPEN WIDE THE GATES

Lord, You have called me to pass through the gates! I choose to prepare the way for the (name) people. I will build up the highway! I will help remove the stones. I will raise a banner for the (name) people. You have anointed me to make Your proclamation to the (name) people. I declare to the (name) people, "See, your Savior comes! See, His reward is with Him, and His recompense accompanies Him." Lord, I give You praise, for the (name) people will be called the Holy People, the Redeemed of the Lord. They will be called Sought After, the City No Longer Deserted. (Isaiah 62:10-12)

O Lord, through my prayers, I will build up and prepare the road and remove the obstacles out of the way of the (name) people. Your Word is like fire and a hammer that breaks a rock in pieces. (Isaiah 57:14; Jeremiah 23:29)

Your word goes out from Your mouth. It will not return to You empty, but will accomplish what You desire and achieve the purpose for which You send it. I thank You for putting Your words in my mouth to uproot and tear down, to destroy and overthrow, to build and to plant in the (name) people. (Isaiah 55:11; Jeremiah 1:9,10)

Thank You, Father, that our struggle is not against flesh and blood, but against the rulers, against the authorities, against the powers of this dark world and against the spiritual forces of evil in the heavenly realms. (Ephesians 6:12)

I declare to the (name) people, "The gods you are worshipping did not make the heavens and the earth. These gods will perish from the earth and from under the heavens. The sacrifices the (name) people offer have been to demons, not to God. The Lord does not want you to be participants with demons. The reason the Son of God appeared was to destroy the devil's work." (Jeremiah 10:11; 1 Corinthians 10:20; 1 John 3:8)

I declare to the rulers, authorities, powers and spiritual forces of evil who have been ruling for centuries over the (name) people: "Lift up your heads, O you gates; be lifted up, you ancient doors, that the King of glory may come in. Who is this King of glory? The Lord strong and mighty, the Lord mighty in battle, the Lord Almighty—He is the King of glory." (Ephesians 6:12; Psalm 24:7-10)

Father, I thank You that when the (name) people cry to You in their trouble, You save them from their distress. I thank You, that You will bring them out of darkness and the deepest gloom and break away their chains. I pray the (name) people will give thanks to You, Lord, for Your unfailing love and Your wonderful deeds for them. Lord, You break down gates of bronze and cut through bars of iron. (Psalm 107:13-16)

Lord, I say to the (name) people, "Be strong, do not fear: your God will come, He will come with vengeance; with divine retribution He will come to save you." To the captives, I say, "Come out," and to those in darkness, "Be Free!" (Isaiah 35:4; 49:9)

O Lord, You will build Your church and the gates of Hades will not overcome it. Almighty God, open the gates that the (name) people may enter. I thank You that Your gates will always stand open, they will never be shut, day or night. (Matthew 16:18; Isaiah 26:2; 60:11,12)

Father, I pray that no longer will violence be heard in the land of the (name) people, nor ruin or destruction within their borders. May the (name) people call their walls Salvation and their gates Praise. (Isaiah 60:18)

THE STRONGHOLD OF THE LORD

Lord, I pray the (name) people would cry to You and say, "You are my refuge, my portion in the land of the living." Father, the (name) people are in desperate need. Rescue the (name) people from those who pursue them, for they are too strong for them. Set the (name) people free from their prison, that they may praise Your name. (Psalm 142:5-7)

Praise You, Lord, that the (name) people have escaped like a bird out of the fowler's snare. The snare has been broken and the (name) people have escaped. Their help is in the name of the Lord, the Maker of heaven and earth. (Psalm 124:6-8)

I thank You, Lord, that You are a refuge for the (name) people who are oppressed. You are a stronghold in times of trouble. The (name) people who know Your name will trust in You, for You, O Lord, have never forsaken those who seek You. (Psalm 9:9,10)

Father, I pray the (name) people will find rest for their souls in You alone. Their hope comes from You. O Lord, You alone are the rock and salvation of the (name) people. You are their fortress. May they not be shaken. Their salvation and honor depend on You, God. Be the mighty rock and refuge of the (name) people. May the (name) people trust in You at all times and pour out their hearts to You, for You are their refuge. (Psalm 62:5-8)

Lord, I pray the (name) people would dwell in Your house all the days of their lives, to gaze upon Your beauty and to seek You in Your temple. For in the day of trouble You will keep the (name) people safe in Your dwelling. You will hide the (name) people in the shelter of Your tabernacle and set them upon a rock. (Psalm 27:4,5)

O Lord, I lift up the (name) people to You. I pray they would trust in You. Do not put them to shame or let their enemies triumph over them. Deliver the (name) people in Your righteousness. Turn Your ear to them. (Psalms 25:1,2; 31:1)

O God, come quickly to their rescue. Be their rock of refuge, a strong fortress to save them and for the sake of Your name lead and guide the (name) people. (Psalm 31:2,3)

Father, be the strength of the (name) people. Be their rock, their fortress and their deliverer. You, Lord, are their shield, the horn of their salvation, their stronghold. When the (name) people call on

You, they will be saved from their enemies for You are an ever-present help in trouble. (Psalms 18:1-3; 46:1)

Lord, You are the light and salvation of the (name) people. Who shall they fear? You, Lord, are the stronghold of the (name) people. (Psalm 27:1)

Great are You, Lord, and most worthy of praise. I thank You that You have shown Yourself to be the fortress of the (name) people. I pray this is the generation of the (name) people who seek You, who seek Your face, O God. (Psalms 48:1-3; 24:6)

ADDITIONAL SCRIPTURES

ADDITIONAL SCRIPTURES

ADDITIONAL SCRIPTURES

RECOMMENDED READING

Becoming A Prayer Warrior, by Elizabeth Alves, published by Renew from Regal, Intercessors International, P.O. Box 390, Bulverde, TX 78163, USA. Phone (830) 438-2615, Fax (830) 438-4215.

International Journal of Frontier Missions, The Adopt-A-People Clearinghouse, P.O. Box 17490, Colorado Springs, CO 80935, USA. Fax (719) 574-7005.

Joshua Project 2000 Unreached Peoples List, AD2000 & Beyond International Office, 2860 S. Circle Drive, #2112, Colorado Springs, CO 80906, USA. Phone (719) 576-2000.

Light the Window: Praying Through the Nations of the 10/40 Window, edited by Floyd McClung, published by YWAM Publishing, P.O. Box 55787, Seattle, WA 98155, USA. Phone (800) 922-2143.

Operation World: The Day-by-Day Guide to Praying for the World, by Patrick Johnstone, published by Zondervan Publishing House, 5300 Patterson Avenue, SE, Grand Rapids, MI 49530, USA.

Possessing the Gates of the Enemy: A Training Manual for Militant Intercession, by Cindy Jacobs, published by Chosen Books, P.O. Box 6287, Grand Rapids, MI 49516, USA.

Prayerwalking: Praying on Site with Insight, by Steve Hawthorne and Graham Kendrick, published by Creation House, Strang Communications Company, 600 Rinehart Road, Lake Mary, FL 32746, USA. Phone (407) 333-3132.

Praying Through the 100 Gateway Cities of the 10/40 Window, edited by C. Peter Wagner, Stephen Peters & Mark Wilson, AD2000 & Beyond, published by YWAM Publishing, P.O. Box 55787, Seattle, WA 98155, USA. Phone (800) 922-2143.

Praying Through the Window III: The Unreached Peoples, edited by Patrick Johnstone, John Hanna and Marti Smith, YWAM Publishing/Caleb Project, YWAM Publishing, P.O. Box 55787, Seattle, WA 98155, USA. Phone (800) 922-2143.

Praying Through the Window IV: Light the Window...Practical Manual for Prayer Journeyers and Home Based Intercessors, published by Christian Information Network, 11005 N. State Highway 83, Colorado Springs, CO 80921, USA. Phone (719) 522-1040.

Strongholds of the 10/40 Window: Intercessor's Guide to the World's Least Evangelized Nations, edited by George Otis, Jr. with Mark Brockman, The Sentinel Group, published by YWAM Publishing, P.O. Box 55787, Seattle, WA 98155, USA. Phone (800) 922-2143.

The Move of the Holy Spirit in the 10/40 Window, by Luis Bush and Beverly Pegues, published by YWAM Publishing, P.O. Box 55787, Seattle, WA 98155, USA. Phone (800) 922-2143.

30 Days Hindu Prayer Focus, an annual "10/40 window" project by WorldChristian News & Books, P.O. Box 26479, Colorado Springs, CO 80936, USA. Phone (719) 442-6469.

30 Days Muslim Prayer Focus, an annual "10/40 Window" project, by WorldChristian News & Books, P.O. Box 26479, Colorado Springs, CO 80936, USA. Phone (719) 442-6469.

Warfare Prayer, a series of books on spiritual warfare and prayer, by C. Peter Wagner, published by Regal Books, Ventura, CA, USA.

WindoWatchman: Praying Through the Window I, by Christian Information Network, 1994, published by Christian Information Network, Colorado Springs, CO 80921, USA. Phone (719) 522-1040.

RECOMMENDED TEACHING TAPES
FROM
INTERCESSORS INTERNATIONAL

Closure, Release and Harvest by Beth Alves. Let go of the past. Learn how to apply closure in areas and to be released to move into the future harvest!

Do You Believe It? by Tommi Femrite. Some of the Lord's promises are easier to believe than others. This two-tape series will help you take an inventory of what you really believe about the Lord and His Word.

Dressing for Revival by Tommi Femrite. God is calling His people to arise and get dressed for the coming revival. Learn about the spiritual clothes He has provided for each of us.

I Am The God Of The Breakthrough by Beth Alves. Has the Lord spoken over you and given you visions and promises? Do you feel like those promises have not been fulfilled or come to fruition? Hear what Beth has to say on this vital topic.

Intercession: Strengthening the Church by Tommi Femrite. This two-tape series explains why pastors need intercessors, how to schedule and guard times of intercession, how to recruit and maintain personal intercessors, qualifications of an intercessor, ways to revive prayer groups, signs of curses and how to break them.

Intercessors Moving Through Their Anointing by Tommi Femrite. As you discover there are different anointings in intercession you will pray with greater confidence and authority. Learning about the different kinds of intercessors will bring greater unity in corporate intercession.

It's Time To Intercede! by Beth Alves. This two-tape series will stir you to intercession. Discover the difference between prayer and intercession. Explore the gifting and fresh anointing for prayer in your life.

More Than Conquerors by Beth Alves. God wants us to triumph in Him. When we walk in Christ Jesus, in the knowledge of Him and in His aroma, we take with us something different.

Passion by Tommi Femrite. God wants people who are passionate for Him and will take that passion into the world. This two-tape series will bring healing and vision. Learn how to deal with things that keep you from being consumed with love for Jesus.

Prophetic Proclamation by Tommi Femrite. Learn more about the power of speaking forth God's Word over a situation, place or nation. Call forth God's plan through prophetic proclamation which moves His hand. Discover how to incorporate prophetic proclamations as you intercede and do spiritual warfare.

Re-Digging The Wells by Tommi Femrite. Discover what stops up your well or the wells in your city. Learn the process of re-digging wells of revival. It's easier to re-dig an old well than dig a new one!

Spiritual Warfare by Tommi Femrite. Learn the keys to victorious warfare in this two-tape series. Topics include identifying the enemy, strategy for warfare, the importance of spiritual armor and how to successfully implement weapons of warfare.

Spiritually Mapping Your City by Beth Alves. Join with others and learn about taking your city through prayer strategy. Focused prayer gets results!

Strongholds by Tommi Femrite. God wants us to come out of the stronghold of darkness and in to the stronghold of light. Deal with personal strongholds in your life before addressing those in nations. It's time to get free!

The Mongolia Trip by Beth Alves and Tommi Femrite. Beth and Tommi share from their hearts in detail on their prayer journey to the heart of the Gobi Desert. Listeners have said, *This is the most powerful tape I've ever heard...I could not drive and listen to this tape at the same time...The anointing is so strong.*

The Spirit of Caleb by Tommi Femrite. Embrace the lifestyle of God's servant who believed the Word of the Lord and held fast to His promises. Call for your inheritance, drive the enemy out and possess the promises of God.

ORGANIZATION AND MINISTRY LISTING

AD2000 & Beyond Movement is committed to reach every person by the year 2000. 2860 S. Circle Drive, #2112, Colorado Springs, CO 80906, USA. Phone (719) 576-2000, Fax (719) 576-2685, Email: info@ad2000.org.

Adopt-a-People Clearinghouse collects unreached people data. P.O. Box 17490, Colorado Springs, CO 80935-7490, USA. Phone (719) 574-7001.

Bethany World Prayer Center collects unreached people groups prayer profiles and distributes them to praying churches and individuals. Attention: Unreached Peoples Project, 13855 Plank Road, Baker, LA 70714, USA. Phone (504) 664-2000, Fax (504) 774-2001, Email: 102132.52@compuserve.com.

Brigada disperses information about missions and unreached people groups through the internet. Email: Brigada,hub@xc.org.

Christian Information Network coordinates the *Praying Through the Window* projects. 11005 State Highway 83, #159, Colorado Springs, CO 80921-3623, USA. Phone (719) 522-1040, Fax (719) 277-7148, Email: CIN@cin1040.com.

Caleb Project gathers information on unreached people groups and mobilization helps. 10 West Dry Creek Circle, Littleton, CO 80120, USA. Phone (303) 730-4170, Fax (303) 730-4177, Email: AdvoNet@cproject.com.

Dawn Ministries focuses on discipling a whole nation. 7899 Lexington Drive, #200-B, Colorado Springs, CO 80920, USA. Phone (719) 548-7460, Fax (719) 54807475, Email: 767731,2145@compuserve.com

Global Harvest Ministries unites prayer networks to maximize prayer power, especially for the 10/40 Window. P.O. Box 63060, Colorado Springs, CO 80962, USA. Phone (719) 262-9929, Fax (719) 262-9920, Email: info@globalharvest.org.

Intercessors International provides training seminars for home based and on-site intercessors. P.O. Box 390, Bulverde, TX 78163, USA. Phone (830) 438-2615, Fax (830) 438-4215, Email: Intercessors_Intl@compuserve.com

The Sentinel Group provides national prayer profiles for countries in the 10/40 Window. P.O. Box 6334, Lynnwood, WA 98036, USA. Phone (206) 627-2989, Fax (206) 672-3028, Email: Sentinelgp@aol.com.

World Prayer Center receives and disperses prayer requests globally with prayer partners and prayer room networks. 11005 Highway 83, #119, Colorado Springs, CO 80921, USA. Phone (719) 262-9922, Fax (719) 262-9920, Email: BByerly@wpccs.org.

YWAM Strategic Frontiers provides training for strategic missions work. P.O. Box 25490, Colorado Springs, CO 80936, USA. Phone (719) 527-9594, Fax (719) 527-2680.